ages
5-7

Houses and homes

Suzanne Kirk

Credits

Author
Suzanne Kirk

Editor
Dulcie Booth

Assistant editor
Roanne Charles

Series designer
Lynne Joesbury

Designer
Catherine Mason

Illustrations
Terry Burton

Cover photographs
Lynne Joesbury

Photographic symbols
History © Stockbyte. Geography and
design & technology © Photodisc, Inc.

Published by Scholastic Ltd,
Villiers House,
Clarendon Avenue,
Leamington Spa,
Warwickshire
CV32 5PR
Printed by Bell & Bain Ltd, Glasgow
Text © Suzanne Kirk
© 2003 Scholastic Ltd
1 2 3 4 5 6 7 8 9 0   3 4 5 6 7 8 9 0 1 2

Visit our website at www.scholastic.co.uk

British Library Cataloguing-in-Publication Data
A catalogue record for this book is available from
the British Library.

ISBN 0-439-98437-8

Contents

Acknowledgements

Photographs
page 5 © 2003, Bryan and Cherry Alexander/alamy.com
pages 6, 10,13,14 & 58 © Scholastic Ltd
page 7 © The Robert Opie Collection
pages 11 & 61 © Nova Developments
pages 16, 17, 24, 36 & 61 © Corel
pages 23 & 27 © Black Country Living Museum, Dudley, West Midlands
page 28 © Getty images/Huton Archive
page 42 © 2003, Nick Dolding/alamy.com
page 50 © Photodisc Inc
page 51 © NASA/Getty Images
page 53 © 2003, Sindre Ellingsen/alamy.com
page 54 © 2003, Bernd Mellmann/alamy.com
page 55 © 2003, Ken Gillham/alamy.com

Introduction

This book provides suggestions and activities covering separate areas of the curriculum which, as a whole, create an exciting and motivating topic which will raise children's awareness of the variety and differences of houses and homes.

The most important place for a young child is their home. It is the place they know best, where the family is, where they keep their belongings, where they feel confident and safe. As their experience widens, children become more aware of other people's homes, different types of homes, homes in places very different to their own locality. During this topic they are encouraged to look around their neighbourhood, to observe, to explore, to ask questions and make connections and comparisons.

Houses and homes brings together aspects of history, geography and design and technology. It will help you create an interesting and relevant topic at Key Stage 1 over a number of weeks which will enable children to find out and learn about different houses and homes in various settings across past and present. There is opportunity for fieldwork in the immediate locality, building models and role-play.

Generally, the activities in each section of *Houses and homes* follow on progressively. Section 3 provides a sequence of activities in which children practise skills and techniques which culminate in making a model. The activities of section 4 gradually introduce children to the concept of island life and the effects and changes this can contribute to an environment, building on their understanding activity by activity.

What subject areas are covered?

This book covers the QCA history unit 2, 'What were homes like a long time ago?', geography unit 3, 'An island home' and design and technology unit 1D, 'Homes'. The topic introduces children to the wide range of different homes today and what homes were like a hundred years ago. It leads on to children applying skills and techniques they have learned to make their own model of a home. Then they focus on the special features relating to an island home. Throughout the book these focal points are intertwined and the learning reinforced.

Teaching specific subject areas through a topic

While it is important to distinguish between the separate subject areas of history, geography and design and technology, natural links can be difficult to ignore and are extremely useful in relating one area of work with another. One subject focus can provide an opportunity to explore another field.

A carefully planned topic can meld together prescribed areas of the curriculum to create interesting learning opportunities appropriate to the needs of the class. Topic-based work presents a whole picture, motivates children and encourages their enthusiasms.

Getting started

Familiarise yourself with the types of houses there are in the immediate neighbourhood. Try to imagine how the children see the area and its houses as they walk along the streets surrounding the school. Make a note of the most common types of homes and the streets where they are located.

Look out also for any unusual and interesting homes. Decide on a suitable route for the children to take when observing the houses of the locality. Locate one or more places to stop where the children can safely observe a range of houses, ask questions and make notes and sketches.

Take photographs which will be valuable as a reference when planning as well as useful when highlighting specific aspects of houses and homes during relevant activities. Ideas for more detailed planning is given in each section. Begin a collection of material relevant to *Houses and homes* and check out useful resources which might be available from museums and historical organisations. (See Resources, below, for a detailed list.)

Involving parents

Involving parents and carers is a useful strategy and can be important in helping to motivate children during their topic work. Adults can encourage children to be more aware of their surroundings when out and about in the neighbourhood. As the interest grows, children will enjoy sharing information and experiences with their parents.

Prepare a letter to parents and carers informing them of the area of work in which their children will be involved. Explain how they can encourage their children to look for different types of houses as they move around the neighbourhood, looking for common and more unusual features of houses. Point out that this can be done in a light-hearted manner through fun activities and normal conversation.

Take this opportunity to ask for the loan of any relevant historical artefacts that the activities would benefit from. Suggest to parents that unbreakable and not particularly valuable items are the most useful.

If appropriate, ask for helpers to accompany the class on fieldwork excursions and to assist in the classroom when the children are making their models.

Resources

Photographs of houses taken in and around the neighbourhood are a valuable resource for this topic of work. Although it is always useful to take photographs when the children are on visits and involved in fieldwork, a bank of photographs taken before the activities begin will provide an extra dimension and an important reference for this work. Photographs can be used where an excursion is not possible and for pointing out or reminding the children of the houses in the locality. They are extremely important for adding value and interest to displays.

Walk around the immediate locality of the school with a list of the types and features of homes you need to photograph. Alternatively, enlist a parent or carer who enjoys photography to help out, providing them with a detailed list of the subjects for pictures. The following photographs would be useful:

Section 1 – different types of houses; close-ups of the external features of homes, such as windows, doors, chimneys, and so on and features which show mathematical shapes, such as rectangular doors and windows, square sides of houses a triangle shape in a roof, a circular window or oval name plaque; more unusual features, such as a balcony or window box; a range of doors or chimneys to make a photo-montage as part of a display; new houses showing modern window frames and doors, bright bricks and tiles and Victorian/Edwardian houses showing original features and decoration

Section 3 – houses being constructed locally.

Further details are given in the preparation and resources sections of each activity.

Historical artefacts are important for children to see and if possible handle. Victorian/Edwardian items are often exhibited in museums and can sometimes be loaned. Find out what is available locally. Often special events or demonstrations can be arranged for children. Particularly useful are washday and cooking items.

Other resources: try to collect as many of the following as possible:
■ a globe
■ a simple map of the British Isles which shows some of the smaller islands
■ material relating to different houses and homes, familiar and more unusual, local and worldwide – pictures, books, video film, estate agents' advertisements
■ material relating to Victorian/ Edwardian home life and showing the interiors of different rooms – pictures, photographs, books, video film
■ pictures of Victorian/Edwardian artefacts
■ resource packs produced by museums and historical organisations on Victorian/Edwardian aspects of home life
■ services provided by museums which encourage children to visit and take part in Victorian/ Edwardian experiences; individuals who visit schools to demonstrate historical artefacts and so on
■ pictures from magazines of modern home interiors
■ camera for taking photographs prior to appropriate activities and for using during fieldwork
■ clipboards for fieldwork
■ a range of construction kits suitable for building models of rooms and houses
■ plane shapes
■ ready-made models of houses
■ art materials for making models, including card, disassembled boxes, masking tape, glue, string, ribbon, wool, collage materials, fabric, transparent materials, paints, crayons, treasury tags, clothes pegs, pipe cleaners, Blu-Tack, paper fasteners
■ tools for artwork, including scissors, snips, rulers, hole-punch, stapler, painting equipment
■ material relating to islands, such as pictures, travel brochures, stories, video film, aerial photographs, especially images of people working, travelling around islands, ferries bringing goods and people
■ for making islands – washing line or skipping rope for island outline; rock and container of water
■ photocopiable pages which can be adapted as appropriate.

Fieldwork opportunities

Section 1 provides valuable opportunities for children to experience working outdoors in the immediate locality. Fieldwork should be enjoyable. Children are understandably excited about leaving the classroom but should know that fieldwork is school work in a different environment, where they can explore, observe, and find out new things for themselves. They should be encouraged to ask questions and give opinions. Work outside the school grounds needs to be very carefully organised:

■ Enlist extra help from other adults so that children can be cared for in small groups.

■ Plan any excursion in detail. Brief all helpers thoroughly. Make sure they know the route to be taken and are clear about procedures for crossing roads. Explain where stops will be made and what the children are expected to do.

■ Make sure the children are well informed about the purpose of the excursion, what they are to look out for, any recording to be done and the behaviour expected of them. Talk about speaking quietly when out, being respectful to people they might meet, taking care especially in busy areas. Remind them about safety issues, particularly involving traffic. Insist they stay close to the adult leader of their group.

■ Carry with you a basic first aid kit, extra pencils and paper, a camera and a mobile phone.

■ Suggest suitable clothing, ensuring the children have hats and gloves when it is cold and sunhats and rainwear as appropriate. Encourage the correct type of shoes for brisk walking.

■ Check LEA guidelines and any particular school guidelines for out-of-school visits.

Introducing the topic to children

Tell the children that they are embarking on an exciting area of work all about houses and homes. Create a sense of discovery. Explain that there will be lots to learn and find out during this topic and many unusual activities to enjoy. There will be opportunities for working out of doors and observing houses and homes in the neighbourhood. Ask the children to keep their eyes open when out and about so as to notice the different types of houses in the area. As they all have a home, they will know a lot about houses and homes already. Be sensitive to any children in the class who have a different home environment, and adapt the way you deliver the activities if necessary so that they don't feel excluded. Explain that there will also be opportunities for making models, and for finding out about people who have their homes in a very different part of the country from themselves.

  Point out to the children that they will be able to look out for books and pictures and discover lots of information for themselves. Suggest that they will be able to use the skills they learn from this topic to make things for themselves at home too.

Suggest the children introduce the theme of the topic to their parents and carers. About this time, inform parents by letter, explaining ways in which they can help (see Involving parents, page 6). Encourage the children to update their families as the topic proceeds, passing on news about the activities they are involved in.

Starting points

It might be useful to elicit the children's initial responses about houses and homes before starting the topic. With little prompting, find out why they think everyone needs a home, what their home means to them and how they think people must feel who do not have a home (again, be sensitive to the circumstances of the children in your class). Ask what they think they will learn from a topic which covers houses and homes.

Homes: now and then

FOCUS

HISTORY
- building a foundation of knowledge and experience of homes today in order to make useful comparisons with the past
- observation of different types of homes in the locality
- examining external features of different homes
- recognising that there are old and new homes

DESIGN AND TECHNOLOGY
- observing different homes and their features as useful preparation for making a model
- recognising mathematical shapes

GEOGRAPHY
- introducing the concept of living on an island

Preparation for section 1

The first four activities of this section require the children to make their own observations of different types of homes and recognise some external features and their shapes. If possible, they should do this as fieldwork in the local area as well as using pictures and specially taken photographs. Children need to see and identify the types of homes common to the neighbourhood, both new and older properties.

Collect pictures and photographs to represent all types of houses, old and new, including estate agents' brochures and the property pages of local newspapers. Look out for homes unusual to the neighbourhood with which the children might not be familiar, such as a block of flats, terraced houses, a mansion. If possible, locate a film showing different types of buildings which the children can identify and discuss.

Depending on the location of the school, it might be possible for the children to make some of their observations from the school grounds, in which case, each of the four activities could be tackled as separate tasks. If planning an excursion around the neighbourhood, it might be appropriate for the children to make all relevant observations for activities 1–4 while away from school. Recording and further discussion can take place in stages back in the classroom.

Preparing for a visit

Familiarise yourself with the housing in the locality and take photographs of as many different types of homes as possible. Plan a walking route where the children can see different types of houses, and decide whether it is better for the children to work in groups or as a whole class. Look for safe and convenient places where they can stop to see, listen, ask questions and make sketches. Perhaps the local park or town-centre square offers views of a range of homes. If necessary, arrange to visit several locations for observing so that the children have identified different homes, compared old and new homes and examined common and unusual external features of homes. Make arrangements with helpers. Before the visit, ensure they understand what the children will be doing and are aware of behavioural codes and safety procedures. Consult LEA guidelines for out of school activities. See 'Fieldwork opportunities' under 'Getting Started' on page 8.

1

**Homes:
now and
then**

HISTORY

DESIGN & TECHNOLOGY

ACTIVITY 1

DIFFERENT HOMES

Learning objective
To be aware that people live in different types of homes.

Resources
Pictures, photographs and perhaps a film showing different types of homes, those typical of the locality as well as others the children might not be familiar with; clipboards and photocopiable page 18 for fieldwork; photocopiable page 19 for classroom recording; pencils and crayons.

Preparation
Plan the fieldwork in which the children will be involved. (See Preparing for a visit, page 9.) Make large, clear labels for the names of different types of homes including *terraced house*, *cottage*, *block of flats*, *semi-detached* and *detached house*; these can be used on a display and the children can refer to them when recording. Before photocopying page 18 write in the names of types of homes you expect the children to observe and draw.

Activity
Show the children a picture or photograph of a home typical of the local area. Do the children know what type of home it is? Perhaps a terraced house, a block of flats, a semi-detached house? Ask if there are any children in the class who live in this type of home. Find out what other types of home the children are familiar with and match their suggestions with examples in pictures or photographs. Ask the children how they would recognise a bungalow, a detached or semi-detached house, a cottage and so on.

   Tell the children that they will be finding out about different types of homes in their neighbourhood. Provide them with photocopiable page 18 on which they can make simple sketches abd/or notes of the four different types of houses you have specified. From the school grounds, or at suitable stopping places when making a visit, ask the children if they can recognise the types of homes and give them the opportunity for making their drawings. Ask questions such as *Are all the homes in this road of the same type? Which type of home have we seen most of? Is it difficult to tell what type of homes some houses are?* If time allows, encourage the children to use the reverse of the photocopiable sheet to draw any other types of homes they have observed.

Back in the classroom, make a list of all the homes the children have identified. Show photographs or a film and discuss any types of houses they were unable to see.

   Look at the list of the types of homes that have been discussed so far. Ask the children if they can think of any other sorts of home people might live in. Challenge them at first to add another five homes to the list. They might think of tent, houseboat, caravan, mobile home, farmhouse, lighthouse and so on. The list can be extended to include homes in other parts of the world such as igloo, hut or cave.

Recording
Children can complete or improve their work on photocopiable page 18 which asks them to draw four types of homes seen in the locality. Then ask them to make a simple drawing of their own home on

photocopiable page 19 and write words or sentences to explain the type of home it is. Afterwards, each child can discuss and compare their house with that of a friend.

Differentiation
Children
- ■ recognise and draw some of the types of homes typical of the neighbourhood
- ■ draw and name different types of homes and compare their own home with others in the locality
- ■ record a wide range of homes and make relevant comparisons.

Plenary
Talk about the types of homes that children have recognised in the neighbourhood. Ask which type of home is the most common. Are there any types of houses not seen in the area? Are there whole streets of one type of home? Which street seems to have the most different types of homes? Discuss the full list of different homes. Did the children think there would be so many?

Display
Arrange photographs and pictures of different types of homes with labels which the children can refer to when recording.

HISTORY   DESIGN & TECHNOLOGY

ACTIVITY 2

FEATURES OF HOMES

Learning objective
To identify external features characteristic to many homes.

Resources
Pictures or photographs showing the external features of different types of homes, such as doors, windows, chimneys and so on; paper; pencils and crayons; Blu-Tack or glue (optional).

Preparation
Check whether the school grounds are a good place for observation. Alternatively, arrange to take a short walk to a nearby spot suitable for observing or make available pictures showing the exteriors of different homes (see Preparation for section 1, page 9). Make a vocabulary list of the names of the features you would like the children to focus on, including *walls*, *roof*, *door*, *windows*, *garage*, *porch*, *steps*, *chimney* and so on as well as any local characteristics.

Activity
Encourage the children to observe carefully one or more homes or pictures of homes. Ask them to tell you the names of the parts of the homes they can see, such as walls, roof, windows, doors, chimney, porch, conservatory, garage and so on. Ask which features all the homes have and which only some of them have. Talk about the shapes and position of windows. Do they have large or small panes of glass? How are the doors different? Perhaps some have glass panels, some painted different colours. If there is a garage, is it joined on to the house or is it a separate building? Can the children tell what materials any of the houses are made of?

Recording

Encourage the children to draw a home, perhaps their own, and to label the features. (They could label their home that they drew on photocopiable page 19 in the previous activity.) They can make their own separate labels, perhaps using the computer, and attach them with Blu-Tack or glue. Alternatively, children can write the names directly onto their drawing. Where appropriate, encourage the children to write descriptive sentences to accompany their drawings, such as *This house has five windows and one green door. The garage is at the side of the house.*

Differentiation

Children:
■ draw the external features of a home they have seen, using labels to identify them
■ use labels to identify the features on their drawing of a home, adding simple sentences
■ draw a house and label the features, adding relevant descriptive sentences.

Plenary

Play a simple game where the children respond by putting their hands up when you name a feature that all homes have (for example, windows) but shaking their heads when the feature is not common to all homes (for example, a garage).

Display

Use the children's drawings together with the photographs and pictures to make a display showing the features of homes. Focus on one feature, perhaps arranging as many images of different doors as possible or creating a montage of chimneys.

ACTIVITY 3

LOOKING FOR SHAPES IN HOMES

DESIGN & TECHNOLOGY

Learning objective

To recognise and name basic mathematical shapes in the context of homes.

Resources

Pictures of the exteriors of houses; plane shapes – rectangles and triangles (different types), squares and circles (different sizes); photocopiable page 20 and clipboards for recording when doing fieldwork; paper; pencils and crayons.

Preparation

Consider if a short walk is necessary or if it is possible to see a range of shapes in the context of the exterior of homes from the school grounds. Especially if fieldwork is not possible, take photographs of good examples of shapes to be seen in homes in the neighbourhood.

Activity

To begin this activity, remind the children of the names of some basic mathematical shapes so they are familiar with their characteristics. Show them different sorts of rectangles and triangles as well as circles and squares of different sizes. Ask them how they will recognise a rectangle and how a square is different. Point out that there are many different types of triangles. Talk about straight lines and curved lines in shapes.

   When observing a house, ask the children what shapes they can see. They will easily recognise the rectangular shapes of doors and windows. Standing directly in front of a house, or using a picture, ask the children to look carefully at the shape of the front wall of the building. Encourage them to trace the outline in the air with a finger. Do they think it is a rectangle or a square? Remind them that a square has all its sides the same length.

Can the children spot any shapes that are triangles? By looking carefully at the roof, they might find such a shape. Is it easy to find circle shapes in houses? Look out for a circular window or a decorative pattern on a house.

Recording
Provide the children with photocopiable page 20 on which they can record some of the shapes they see in houses, either as small drawings or as written descriptions. Provide the children with a selection of plane shapes and ask them to make a home using only the shapes. Tell them to think carefully about using the most appropriate sizes of the shapes. Can they draw a house which has all four shapes – rectangle, square, triangle and circle? The children can write the names of the shapes as labels on their drawing or write sentences of explanation: *The door is a rectangle. The blue window is a square. The yellow window is a rectangle and the green window is a circle.* If appropriate, the children can make lists writing the features they have drawn under headings – square, rectangle, circle, triangle.

Differentiation
Children:
■ use shapes to draw a representation of a house, writing the names to identify the shapes
■ draw a house using shapes, considering appropriate sizes and adding sentences which describe the shapes and features
■ draw a house using shapes and sizes appropriately, writing sentences of explanation and making a chart which sorts the shapes.

Plenary
Discuss which shapes were the most easy to spot. Was this because there were more of these than the others? What was the biggest rectangle they saw? Was there a shape that could not be found? Encourage the children to keep looking for shapes when they are out and about and then report back.

Display
Draw a large representation of a house with labels to indicate the names of the shapes and corresponding features. Display the children's pictures of shape houses.

HISTORY

ACTIVITY 4

HOMES: OLD AND NEW

Learning objective
To understand that homes were built differently in the past and had features which look different from those of houses today.

Resources
Pictures and video footage (optional) of relatively new homes and homes in the process of being built, especially photographs of local examples; pictures and photographs of Victorian/ Edwardian homes, especially any in the neighbourhood and old photographs showing houses when occupied in Victorian or Edwardian times; an old brick and a new brick; photocopiable page 21; pencils and crayons.

Preparation
Check out suitable houses for the children to observe. Find an obviously newly built home where the brickwork is not weathered and the windows and doors are of typically modern

style. To compare with the new house, locate a Victorian or Edwardian home where the bricks appear old and the doors and windows are wooden and more traditional. If possible, choose examples of homes belonging to children in the class and ask parents' permission to stand outside and make observations. If easily accessible examples are unavailable, locate a video film and large, clear pictures.

Activity

From the school grounds or on a visit around the neighbourhood, draw the children's attention to both new and older types of houses. Ask how the children can tell if a house is quite new. Suggest that they look for clues. Examine the building materials, for example. Can the children describe the brickwork? Perhaps it is bright and clean-looking. What about the windows? Is it possible to tell how they open? What are the window frames made of? Is the front door made of the same material as the windows? Perhaps the garage has been built as part of the house. Try to get the children to comment on the style of the home. Perhaps it has a simple, plain look about it and a newly planted garden.

Next, look at an older house. What is the brickwork like? What makes it look old? Talk about the years the home has stood in rain, wind and frost. Are the windows different from the newer home? What are they made of and how do they open? Perhaps the door has patterns; perhaps it has panels of old glass. Encourage comments on the style and the 'feel' of the home. It might be of a dull appearance, and have decorative details. Ask the children how old they think the home is. Explain that it could be a hundred years old. If appropriate, suggest the children think of and remember three differences they have noticed between the old and the new house to recall when back at school.

If suitable homes are not within a convenient distance of the school, it will be necessary to rely on photographs and pictures for the children to make their observations and comparisons. Point out that many old houses today have been altered and given modern features by their owners.

Back in the classroom, show the children an old photograph or an illustration of a Victorian or Edwardian house. Explain that this house which would be old now, was once a new house. Ask the children what clues tell them that it is not a modern house. Remind them of a modern house with which they are familiar and ask them to recall the differences they remembered earlier between modern and old houses. Perhaps they will notice the style and shape of some of the features as different from those of houses built today? They might comment on the windows, garden, a smoking chimney. Ask the children if anything is missing from the Victorian house. There will not be a garage, television aerial or satellite dish. Show the children the old and the new brick and point out that although people often like to give old houses new doors and windows, the bricks usually remain and give a clue to the age of the home.

Recording

Give the children photocopiable page 21 which provides outlines of an old and modern house. Ask the children to complete these pictures by making one house look as if it were built about a hundred years ago and the other as if it were recently built. Tell them to think carefully about the types of doors and windows they will give each house, whether each house will have chimneys. Suggest the new house is given a garage, an aerial and satellite dish. Alternatively, children can create their own pictures which show the differences between an old and a new home.

Differentiation
Children
■ recognise and draw some of the features of old and new homes
■ distinguish between old and new homes, adding relevant features to their drawings and making comparisons
■ make appropriately labelled drawings of a Victorian/Edwardian home and a modern home and write sentences to explain the differences between the two types of home.

Plenary
Talk about the houses most common to the area around the school. Are they mostly older houses or are they newly built? Perhaps there are both types? Do most of the children live in one type of home? Which children would like to live in a brand new house if they had the choice?

Display
Create a display which compares old and new homes. Use pictures and make available books about homes in Victorian/Edwardian times. Contrast this with pictures and books of modern homes and homes in the process of construction. Use local examples where possible. Add the children's work as appropriate.

GEOGRAPHY   DESIGN & TECHNOLOGY

ACTIVITY 5

WHAT TYPE OF HOME WOULD YOU LIKE?

Learning objectives
To collect and communicate information; to identify likes and dislikes and respect others' opinions.

Resources
Photocopiable page 22; paper; pencils and crayons.

Preparation
Have available pictures and photographs from the previous activities to refer to when talking about different types of homes such as a bungalow, block of flats and so on.

Activity
Begin by asking the children what type of home they would like to live in if they had the choice. Give them the opportunity to be imaginative and uninhibited. Then ask questions relating to the choices on photocopiable page 22 so that they will more easily understand the text when they come to use it. What size house would they like as a home? Point out that the larger the home the more there is to keep clean. Discuss the merits of living in a bungalow, a two-storey house and a high-rise flat. Perhaps some children will comment on the splendid view from a tall building. If they could choose, who would prefer to live in a town, in the countryside, by the sea? Talk briefly about the materials of which the home might be built. Would they prefer brick, stone or a wooden house like a log cabin? Refer to the previous activity and remind the children about old and new houses. Move on to talk about special

features a home might have. Try to restrict the children to talking about external features and suggest some of the features a particular home might have, such as a flagpole, balcony, garden and garage.

Recording

Show the children photocopiable page 22 and tell them that it can be used to show others what type of home they would like. Explain that they should draw a circle around the words which describe the home they would like and that they should circle only one description in each of the five sections at the top. It might be appropriate for the children to work simultaneously in a group while the words are read out to them. For the second part of the page, ask the children to circle the three features they would most like to have as part of their home.

   When the choices have been made, the children can exchange their pages of information and draw another's favoured type of home. Help them to imagine they are designers or architects, who can produce a picture to show someone the type of home they would like. Some children might like to write sentences to explain the features of their drawing: *This house is for Sam. He would like to live in a bungalow by the sea. It will be new and made of wood with a flagpole, garage and conservatory.*

Differentiation

Children:
- make and indicate their choices for a home
- design a home following given specifications, providing a heading and simple written explanation
- can follow another's instructions for designing a home, writing a detailed description.

Plenary

Discuss some of the pictures of houses drawn to the children's specifications. Ask if the design of the house is what was expected. Has the architect followed the instructions? Is the client happy with the design?

Display

Make a wall display or a book which shows the choices circled on the photocopiable sheet next to the drawings and their descriptions.

ACTIVITY 6

ISLAND LIFE

GEOGRAPHY

Learning objective

To become aware that living on a small island is quite different from living on the mainland.

Resources

Pictures, a video film, travel brochures and books which illustrate travelling to an island.

Preparation

Draw a simple representation of an island, using pictures and words to demonstrate some of its features.

   For children who do live on an island, the activity will need to be adapted so that life on the mainland is described.

Activity

Begin by asking the children to tell you anything they know about islands. Then use the information they give to establish that an island is a relatively small piece of land surrounded by water, probably the sea. Draw a representation of a small island as you talk, showing the mainland in relation to the island. Perhaps the children can think of a name for the island you have created.

Move on to discuss how to get to the island and what it might be like living there. Point out that only a few people could live on such a small piece of land.

Emphasise three main points about island life:

1. Explain that many things we take for granted would not be available on a small island. There might only be one shop and perhaps a very small school. Tell the children about the things they are used to which would not be available on a small island. Refer to facilities in the children's locality, such as the library, shops, fast food places and sports facilities. Would the children mind having to do without these things if they lived on a small island?

2. Next, ask the children how they would feel about travelling by small boat every time they needed to visit friends, shops, the cinema, perhaps even to get to school. Would it be pleasant in winter, in the dark, when the sea was rough? Briefly compare travelling to the mainland with the methods of travel the children are familiar with.

3. Finally, emphasise the peacefulness of living on a small island. Get the children to imagine life without busy roads, traffic, crowds of people, everyday noise they are used to. Briefly talk about animals there might be on the island and in the sea such as seals, fish and birds. Make references to the children's experience of everyday life in their neighbourhood and point out the differences.

Give the children the opportunity to talk about reasons why they would like to live on a small island as well as why they might not want to have their home there.

Recording

Suggest the children draw a small island of their own. Perhaps they could show where they would have their home and what else there might be. Do not encourage too much detail at this stage. Then ask the children to complete the sentences *I would like to live on an island because…* and *I would not like to live on an island because…* Encourage them to give their own opinions and reasons.

Differentiation

Children:
■ draw a representation of an island and understand that living there is different from their way of life
■ draw an island and use words or sentences to record their opinions of island life and what life is like there
■ draw and label an island and describe in sentences the advantages and disadvantages of living there.

Plenary

Look at the children's pictures and the reasons they have given. Talk about the advantages of living on an island and compare them with the advantages of living where they do now. Consider the disadvantages of each place too. Do most children prefer their present way of life?

Display

Display the large picture you have drawn to represent an island (see Preparation, above). Perhaps add extra features such as a whale swimming offshore, someone fishing, a small boat ferrying people and supplies. Make available books describing island life.

HISTORY   DESIGN & TECHNOLOGY

Different homes

Draw four different homes that you have seen.

■SCHOLASTIC

HISTORY   DESIGN & TECHNOLOGY

Photocopiable

What type of house do you live in?

Draw a picture of your house.

What type of house is it?

_____

_____

_____

_____

MSCHOLASTIC

DESIGN & TECHNOLOGY

Looking for shapes in homes

What shapes are there in the homes that you have seen? Draw and/or write about them in the right shape.

Homes: old and new

Make this house new.

Make this house old.

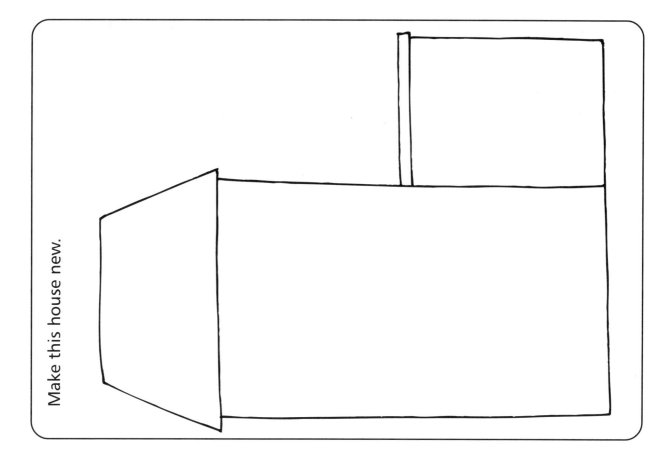

What type of home would you like?

Choose one thing from each row.

small	medium	large
two storeys	high-rise flat	bungalow
in a town	in the country	by the sea
made of bricks	made of stone	made of wood
new	old	very old

Which of these would you like your home to have? You can choose any three.

tower	flagpole	conservatory
balcony	garden	swimming pool
garage	shed	pond

Inside homes: now and then

FOCUS

HISTORY

■ comparing the interiors of homes of Victorian or Edwardian times with those of today

■ using household items from the past to find out how people lived

■ discovering how changes in the interiors of homes have affected the way we live

DESIGN AND TECHNOLOGY

■ creating a simple model to represent a room of a hundred years ago

Preparation for section 2

For these activities it is important to try to create for the children an experience which represents life in Victorian or Edwardian times. Collect books, pictures and video films which show the home life of an average family about one hundred years ago. Historical organisations often supply resource packs compiled especially for children. Local museums sometimes provide relevant displays and interactive experiences for children where they can take part in Victorian activities, dressing up, using household items, and immersing themselves in role-play. Museums will also sometimes loan household artefacts for use in schools. Parents and grandparents of the children are often willing to allow family possessions and photographs to be brought to school for a display. A letter sent home explaining that children will be finding out about life in homes one hundred years ago and asking for help will usually encourage families to hunt out their treasures. It is useful if the school acquires its own basic collection of household items for the children to examine.

If appropriate, make plans to create a Victorian or Edwardian room in a corner of the classroom where the children can enact family life a hundred years ago.

Supplied by Black Country Living Museum, Dudley, West Midlands

HISTORY

ACTIVITY 1

INSIDE OUR HOMES

Learning objective
To know that changes have occurred inside our homes which affect the way we live.

Resources
A set of pictures or video film showing the interior of an average Victorian or Edwardian home; pictures from magazines showing the interior of modern homes; photocopiable page 31; pencils.

Preparation
If the children are to see a video film, decide which are the appropriate places to stop the tape so that they can comment and ask and answer questions.

Activity
Show the children pictures or a video film of the interior of a typical Victorian or Edwardian home. Tell them that people would have lived in a home like this about a hundred years ago. It might be useful to explain that a hundred years ago is a long time ago, before their parents, grandparents and great-grandparents were born, but not nearly as long ago as when people lived in caves or wooden huts. Very old people will have heard from their parents what homes were like a hundred years ago.

Suggest the children look for clues to tell them what each room is used for. Can they identify the kitchen (which would have probably been called a scullery), the living room, bedroom, the room which would have been known as the parlour and today we might call a lounge? Is there a special room for washing and bathing? What are the bedrooms like? Where is the toilet?

If necessary, use photographs of the interiors of modern homes to help the children make comparisons. Ask them what they notice in a Victorian home which is different from the inside of their own home. Encourage them to discuss the style of furniture, the colour schemes, the furnishings, the heating and lighting. Why do the children think there is a fireplace in every room? Discuss the things which are absent from the Victorian home, such as a television, washing machine and other electrical equipment. Are there any children's toys or possessions to be seen? Do the children think they would have felt 'at home' in such a house?

Recording
Provide the children with photocopiable page 31 which shows some features of homes. Read these with the children and then ask them to indicate by ticks and crosses, or writing yes or no, in the boxes which of the things people would have had in their homes a hundred years ago. They can complete the page by writing sentences to comment on an aspect of home life one hundred

years ago which they would not enjoy. For example, *I would not like to go outside to the toilet, especially in the wintertime. There would be no electricity and no television.*

Differentiation
Children:
■ indicate some of the differences between homes today and those a hundred years ago
■ distinguish between features in homes a hundred years ago and those today, writing words or sentences to explain and comment upon what they would not enjoy about living in such a home
■ compare features in homes a hundred years ago with those today, writing detailed explanations and comments to show how life has changed.

Plenary
Read out some of the comments the children have made in their recording. Do others agree? What would the children think they might dislike the most? Is there anyone who would have enjoyed home life one hundred years ago?

Display
Arrange pictures of modern rooms along side those of Victorian or Edwardian rooms. Use the computer to print out some of the children's comments to add to the display.

ACTIVITY 2

HISTORY

HOME LIFE A HUNDRED YEARS AGO

Learning objective
To understand how life in the home has changed since Victorian or Edwardian times.

Resources
Pictures, books and video films of household items and furniture from the Victorian or Edwardian periods, especially relating to washday and cooking activities; artefacts or replicas for the children to handle and examine, for example a heavy old saucepan, cooking pots, metal bucket, old pottery and bottles, a tray with embroidered cloth, teapot with knitted cosy, china cup and saucer, a clothes horse and wicker clothes basket, old type of pegs, wash tub and ponch, brush and dustpan and so on; photocopiable page 32; pencils and crayons.

Preparation
Make labels for each artefact and any pictures used, so the children can identify them as well as using the vocabulary when recording.

Activity
Show the children a selection of Victorian or Edwardian household items and ask them if they can tell what they are. Consider all suggestions, emphasising any clues which the children have used to help in the identification. Then begin to talk about how each item was used and which room it would most likely to have been needed in. Focus on washday activities in the scullery or cooking in the living room where the range would be and use pictures when talking about items such as a mangle or cooking range. Refer to the equivalent items we use today as well as stressing the inconvenience we would find in relying on many of the household objects which people had one hundred years ago.

Show the children a photograph of a cooking range which would have once been the focal point in a home. Discuss the different parts, where the oven is and the fire which provides the heat. Can the children tell from the picture how the water in the kettle is boiled, where the cooking pans are heated and the bread is baked? What is the fuel and where is it stored? Perhaps there is a bucket of coal beside the range. Before a meal could be cooked the fire would have to be made with wood and paper and kept stoked with coal. Describe how this process of heating and cooking would make the room warm but dusty, with coal dust and ash floating through the air. Explain how a dustpan and brush would always be ready, next to the fireplace, for sweeping up and the cooking range itself would need lots of cleaning.

  Encourage the children to make comparisons with the methods of cooking and baking in their home. Very few homes will use coal or wood today, but will have a gas supply or use electricity which are much cleaner fuels. The cookers themselves are smaller and are easy to clean. Microwave ovens help us to save time.

Recording
Show the children photocopiable page 32 with the outline of the cooking range. Ask them to complete this picture by putting in the fire and adding cooking equipment, such as a kettle and saucepans on the hob. They can show bread baking or meat roasting in the oven. Remind them to provide a bucket of coal and a brush and dustpan for sweeping up. You can also suggest including clothes drying close by and a cat sleeping near the warm hearth. On the second half of the page, ask the children to make a drawing of the cooker in their own home with accompanying sentences explaining how it is used. The reverse of the page can be used to continue comments.

Differentiation
Children:
■ represent by drawing, modern and older styles of cooking
■ show through drawings and words or sentences, some differences between cooking methods today and those a hundred years ago
■ provide details in drawings and sentences comparing cooking today with that a hundred years ago.

Plenary
Talk about how much easier it is to make a cooked meal today than it was a hundred years ago. Remind the children of the lengthy procedures which people had to carry out and ask them to provide today's equivalent action. For example, compare *Get up very early to make the fire. Wait while it heats up. Fill the kettle with water and put it on the hob to boil.* with *Get up and switch on the electric kettle and the water boils in a few minutes.*

Display
Collect together labelled items and pictures which represent cooking or washing in Victorian or Edwardian times which the children can examine.

HISTORY

ACTIVITY 3

NEW AND OLD

Learning objective
To be aware that many of the things we use in our homes today are different from a hundred years ago.

Resources
Household items from Victorian or Edwardian times including a flat iron, candle in holder, a jug and bowl, a pen with a nib and a bottle of ink; pictures showing examples of household items in use; photocopiable page 33; pencils and crayons.

Preparation
Select the objects to be discussed; if photocopiable page 33 is to be used, choose a flat iron, candle holder, jug and bowl and pen and ink.

Activity
Show the children a light bulb and draw their attention to the classroom lighting. Demonstrate how easy it is to provide light when it is needed by using the switches to obtain electricity. Then consider what the Victorians/Edwardians might have used to light their homes. Explain that they would have some light from their coal fire but most people would have used candles to read, sew or write after dark. When moving from room to room and going upstairs, they would need a special holder for the candle. Show the children a candle-holder with a handle and drip tray and discuss the inconvenience of having to hold the light while moving about. Discuss also how dangerous it could be and emphasise that the light produced would be quite dim. Point out that although we often use candles today, it is mainly for decorative purposes; we do not have to rely on their light.

Next, show the children an old flat iron and explain how it would be used; that it needed to be heated near the fire, or on the hob, before smoothing the creases from clothes. Give the children the opportunity to feel the weight of the iron and comment on the metal of which it is made. Do they think it would be easy to use? Would it stay warm? Does the iron used in their home stay hot while it is needed? Is it as heavy?

Demonstrate how to use a pen with a nib by dipping it into a bottle of ink. Explain that in Victorian times this was the only method of writing letters or instructions in the home and the writing equipment would be put away carefully in a drawer when not being used. Do the children think their work would be as neat as when they use a felt-tipped pen or ballpoint pen? Why does a writer with a nib pen have to keep stopping?

Talk about the function of a jug and bowl in a Victorian or Edwardian home, how people washed in their bedrooms, usually with cold water, then took the dirty water outside to dispose of it. Then ask someone to describe where they wash their hands and face each morning, what they use and how they get rid of their dirty water.

Discuss any other items as appropriate.

Recording
Provide the children with photocopiable page 33 which has pictures of modern household items – a steam iron, light bulb, wash basin and felt-tipped pens. Ask the children to draw and name the equivalent objects as used a hundred years ago. Encourage them to refer to the artefacts which have been used in discussion. If appropriate, the reverse of the page can be used for children to describe the differences and make comparisons.

Supplied by Black Country Living Museum, Dudley, West Midlands

Differentiation
Children:
■ make drawings to show the differences between household items now and a hundred years ago
■ compare modern and old household items and describe in words and sentences how life has changed
■ show the differences between modern and old household items, providing a detailed description of the changes in lifestyles.

Plenary
Encourage the children to give their impressions of life at home one hundred years ago. How does it compare with their home life? Do they think it would be less comfortable and convenient to use a jug and bowl for washing, a candle for lighting and pen and ink when writing? Is it quicker to do things today?

HISTORY

ACTIVITY 4

A ROOM A HUNDRED YEARS AGO

Learning objective
To become familiar with key features of rooms long ago and today.

Resources
Video film, books and pictures which show different rooms in Victorian or Edwardian times; photocopiable page 34; pencils and crayons.

Preparation
Decide which room of the house the children will focus on. This might be determined by the resources available. The whole class can focus on the same room or groups of children can focus on different rooms, for example the scullery, living room, parlour or bedroom. If appropriate, make arrangements for the children to take part in any Victorian or Edwardian experiences at a local museum.

Activity
Present the children with examples of the room or rooms on which you want them to focus. Ask questions which encourage the children to look for clues as to the activities which take place in the rooms.

Living room – the table shows that this is where the family sit together for their meals; the cooking range that the meals are also cooked in this room which will usually be warm and cosy. Perhaps the children can spot that the washing is aired in this room too. Are there differences between this home and a home today? Perhaps the children will explain that food is cooked in the kitchen at their home, not where the family sit. This means that if there is a fire in their living room at home, it will be of quite a different design.

Scullery – explain that homes a hundred years ago had a small room where the sink was which was called a scullery. What do the children think happened in this room? Briefly discuss washing arrangements, referring to the previous activity if appropriate, and help the children to understand that washday really did last all day – heating the water, boiling or scrubbing the clothes, squeezing out water with the mangle and getting rid of the dirty water. Emphasise what a lengthy, tiring and messy task washing would be. Compare this with laundry arrangements in the children's homes today.

Bedroom – make the children aware of how bare a Victorian or Edwardian bedroom would be compared with their own. Apart from sleeping, probably the only other activity would be washing using the jug and bowl. The room would be cold most of the time, with a fire being lit only when a child was ill. Contrast this with the children's cosy, colourful bedrooms which are probably filled with toys and electrical equipment.

Parlour – explain that many Victorian or Edwardian homes would have a room they called a parlour. This was only used on special occasions or when visitors came to call. From pictures, can the children suggest what this room was used for? The sofa and chairs show that people sat there. As there are probably no toys, what would the children in those days do if they were allowed in? Talk about the decoration of the room. What are the children's general impressions? How is the room different from a similar room in their house? Perhaps they would agree it has a similar use to the lounge in their home.

© Getty images/Hulton Archive

Recording

Tell the class or groups of children which room they are to focus on and ask them to use photocopiable page 34 to make a drawing of this room and a drawing of the equivalent room in their own home. As appropriate, they can label the features of each room or write words or sentences which explain the differences. *My bedroom is warmer and brighter than a child's bedroom a hundred years ago. We sit in our lounge every day.* Write in the titles of the rooms to be drawn, or leave this for the children to complete.

Differentiation

Children:
■ draw a room in their own home and the equivalent one in a home a hundred years ago showing some of the differences
■ compare the drawings they have made, writing sentences to describe the differences
■ show in detail in their drawings and writing how a room in their home is different from an equivalent home a hundred years ago.

Plenary

Talk about the overall impression the children have acquired of homes a hundred years ago and compare it with their own experience of home – that today homes are warmer, brighter and more colourful. Do the children think that homes today are more comfortable? Do they as children have more belongings? Would anyone prefer to have lived in a home as it was a hundred years ago?

DESIGN & TECHNOLOGY   HISTORY

ACTIVITY 5

MAKING A MODEL ROOM

Learning objective

To practise some joining techniques by making a simple model of a room as it would be a hundred years ago.

Resources

Thin card; masking tape; glue; paints; crayons; collage materials including fabric and wallpaper pieces; modelling materials; scissors.

Preparation

Decide whether the children will all focus on the same room or whether groups will each represent a different room, for example a bedroom, living room, scullery or parlour.

Depending on the ability of the children and the availability of materials and tools, plan the procedure for making the models.

For each child, cut two pieces of card – one for the base (25cm × 20cm) and the other for the walls (42cm × 12cm). The card for the walls should be scored or marked for the children to score (see diagram).

Adjust measurements for bigger or smaller rooms accordingly.

Assess and minimise the risks which arise when using sharp tools.

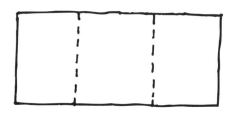
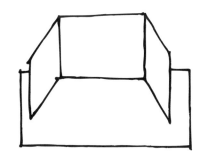

2

Activity

Referring to resources relating to rooms in a Victorian or Edwardian house and to the previous activity, talk to the children about the room they will build. Explain that the room will have just three sides so that it will be easy to work with and people will be able to see the detail of the inside.

Show the children how the room will be constructed. Demonstrate how one piece of card can be folded into three to make the back and side walls. If appropriate show the children how they can score the card to make folds, otherwise present them with ready-scored card. Explain how the second piece of card represents the ground and is larger than the floor space required so that the model can be handled easily and labelled. Discuss how the two pieces of

card could be fastened together. Have the children any suggestions? Then show the children how to make simple hinges from small pieces of card and glue or by using masking tape. Is one large hinge a good idea or is it better to have several smaller ones?

Tell the children they will need to work on their rooms in four stages:

1. The walls should be decorated by drawing in windows with curtains, and perhaps a doorway. Some features can be drawn directly onto the card or drawn separately, cut out and glued onto the walls. Children might like to create wallpaper for their room and make a shelf out of card using the same technique as used for making a hinge. Talk about the features they will need to include for their particular room. Encourage them to refer to books and pictures for ideas and details.

Living room – children draw a cooking range with pots and pans; mantlepiece above with household items such as a candlestick, vase, photograph; clothes airing on a line, pictures on the wall, shelves.

Scullery – the walls will not be decorated, but will have pots and pans hanging up as well as shelves perhaps with food on them; there will be a sink, perhaps a table.

Bedroom – the walls will be wallpapered; there might be a picture and mirror on the wall; the washstand with jug and bowl can be represented by a drawing.

Parlour – wallpaper on the walls with pictures and photographs of relatives on the walls; perhaps a pot plant.

2. Attach the walls to the base using hinges.

3. Add furniture such as a bed, table, or chairs which can be made from card or modelled from clay, Plasticine or a similar material.

4. Complete the model by writing a title on the base to tell people about the room they have made: *This is a model of a Victorian bedroom made by…*

Differentiation

Children:

■ construct a model room from prepared card using simple joining methods, then furnish the room

■ construct a model of a room, scoring folds and making hinges for joining purposes, furnishing the room appropriately with collage materials and simple models

■ construct a model of a room using scoring and joining techniques, decorating the room in detail using a variety of methods and providing handmade furniture.

Plenary

Discuss the models. Encourage the children to admire details in each other's work. Look for particularly stable constructions and advise others where improvements might be made.

Display

Arrange the models where they can be safely admired and talked about informally by the children. Display books and pictures near by so that parents and visitors can appreciate what the children aimed to achieve.

Inside our homes

Which of these things would you have had in your home a hundred years ago?

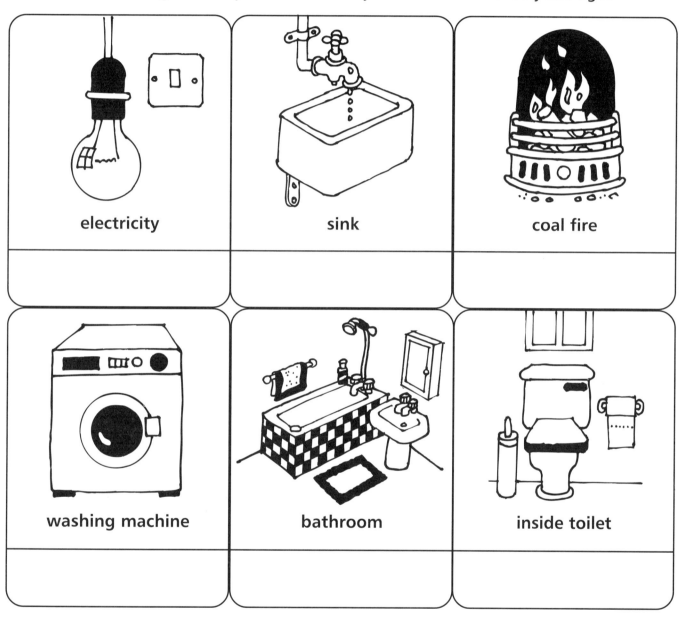

electricity

sink

coal fire

washing machine

bathroom

inside toilet

What wouldn't you have liked a hundred years ago?

_____

_____

_____

SCHOLASTIC

Home life a hundred years ago

Complete the picture of the cooking range.

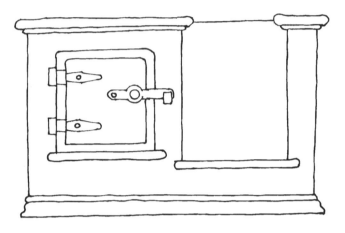

Cooking in my home

HISTORY

■SCHOLASTIC

New and old

What would have been used a hundred years ago instead of these modern items? Draw the old items in the boxes and name them.

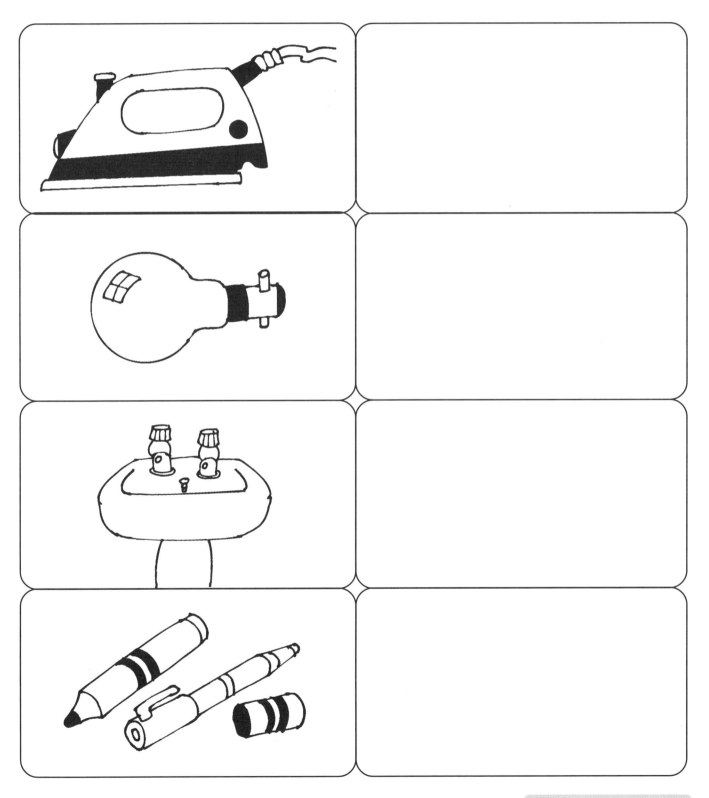

A room a hundred years ago

A hundred years ago

Today

Building a model of a home

FOCUS

DESIGN & TECHNOLOGY

DESIGN AND TECHNOLOGY
- everyone's need for a home
- activities leading up to building a model home:
  - shapes of the features of houses
  - fastening and joining 2-D and 3-D materials
  - making structures more stable
  - planning and making

HISTORY

HISTORY
- different types of homes

Preparation for section 3

The activities in this section prepare children for building their own model of a house, beginning with understanding everyone's need for private space for themselves and their family. If appropriate, provide the children with the opportunity to create a mini-home for themselves which could involve den-building in the school grounds or experience with natural materials at an outdoor activity centre. With the children, devise a reading tent in a corner of the classroom or corridor, where they can take turns to claim their own space and escape from the rest of the class for a quiet reading session. The tent can be decorated inside with pictures of characters from books or remain quite plain to give the idea of seclusion.

As the children become involved in the activities of this section, encourage them to find out extra things for themselves, such as different houses around the world (perhaps those seen on holidays or on television) and homes of pets and wild creatures. Admire any models and drawings the children are motivated to make at home.

The activities in this section enable the children to accumulate skills and build on experience in order to plan and make their own model in activities 6 and 7. Ideally the activities should follow progressively leading up to the model making.

Preparation for model making

Collect together materials including construction kits, empty boxes which can be disassembled so the blank sides can be used, different types of card, adhesive tape and glues, collage materials. Also needed are scissors, rulers, paints and other finishing materials.

Decide on the organisation of the class, the space available for working and storing the models while they are being made, the time required and the number of sessions needed for the model-making activities. It might be appropriate for the children to work on consecutive days when making the model, rather than spread out the process which could diminish their enthusiasm.

Decide to what degree of detail the children should make their models, which will depend on ability and perhaps time available. Some children will make a simple, painted model from boxes while others might be inspired to make a more detailed model which shows a furnished interior and includes a garden.

If appropriate, organise parents as helpers when making sessions are in progress. Take steps to minimise risks when children are using sharp tools.

3

Building a model of a home

DESIGN & TECHNOLOGY

HISTORY

ACTIVITY 1

EVERYONE NEEDS A HOME

Learning objectives
To understand how and why we enclose space, and the need to make a home. To realise that people live in different sorts of homes.

Resources
Pictures and models of a wide range of homes, such as tent, cave, igloo, log cabin, straw house, mud hut, brick and stone homes, tree house and so on; photocopiable page 45.

Preparation
Consider making a reading tent in the classroom or corridor (see Preparation for section 3, page 35); if appropriate, organise a den-building experience for the children.

Activity
Ask the children to tell you why they need a home. Reasons should include a place to live, to shelter, to sleep, to prepare food and to eat, somewhere to keep things, somewhere for the family to be together. Discuss the importance of having a home; that 'going home' is usually something to look forward to. Encourage the children to talk about what their home means to them. Talk about whether the children feel the need to make a den or similar structure to enclose their own space, like a mini-home. Ask the children to tell you about dens they have made in their gardens or indoors, perhaps under a table. Suggest the children think of ideas for making a special private reading space somewhere in the classroom.

Move on to consider different ways of making a home to provide a family with a private space. Point out that in some parts of the world a home shelters people from the heat whereas in other parts people need somewhere to keep warm. Ask the children to tell you what materials people might use to make this special place. They might mention bricks, stone, concrete and wood and then think of more unusual materials including mud, straw, ice, fabric, metal and so on. Use pictures to show the children homes made from these materials, such as an igloo, tent and thatched hut. Point out that a cave is a ready-made home.

Recording
Ask the children to make appropriate drawings to go with the phrases on photocopiable page 45 which give reasons why people need a home. For example, they could draw a bedroom to show *somewhere to sleep safely*. The children can depict themselves in their own home or in an imaginary home where they would like to be. They should add a personal comment in words or sentences explaining their own need for a home.

Differentiation
Children:
■ make simple drawings to show some reasons why people need a home
■ make drawings to represent the reasons why people need homes, adding words or simple sentences to give a personal comment
■ make drawings to represent why people need homes, adding informed sentences to make a personal comment.

CURRICULUM LINKS ages 5–7: Houses and homes

Plenary

Ask the children to tell each other what it means to them to have a home. Point out the importance of having a home whatever material it is made from. Briefly mention people in some parts of the world who have lost their homes because of disasters such as flooding or an earthquake. Point out that what they want most is somewhere safe to live. Suggest that the children can find out more for themselves about different types of homes, including homes for pets and the sort of homes wild creatures choose.

Display

Arrange the pictures and models of different homes as well as the children's completed photocopiable sheets.

ACTIVITY 2

MAKING A CHAIN

DESIGN & TECHNOLOGY

Learning objective

To practise ways of fastening 2-D materials together.

Resources

Thin card; wool, pipe cleaners or fine string; treasury tags; paper fasteners; Blu-Tack; glue; masking tape; clothes pegs; hole punch; scissors; crayons.

Preparation

Cut pieces of thin card – sizes could be 12cm x 6cm (one piece per child) and 8cm x 10cm (at least three pieces per child). As a demonstration, write the word *Homes* in large colourful letters on the 12cm x 6cm piece of card and represent, with a simple drawing and a label, a different type of home on three of the other sized pieces. If time allows, the title can be repeated and other homes represented on the reverse of the cards.

Activity

Refer to the different homes in the previous activity 'Everyone needs a home', if appropriate, and show the children the cards you have prepared with drawings of different homes. Tell them you are going to attach them to each other to make a chain which you can then hang up as a decoration and to give information. The word *Homes* will be at the top and the other cards will hang beneath. Ask the children if they have any ideas for fastening the cards to each other. Listen carefully to all suggestions and show the children the tools and materials you have gathered together for this activity. If necessary, this might provide them with clues.

Demonstrate some ideas for fastening pieces of card together. Remind, or show, the children how to make hinges using card and glue or masking tape. Show them how to make a neat hole with a hole punch and use wool, fine string or pipe cleaners to tie the cards loosely together. Then demonstrate how a treasury tag or paper fastener can also be used.

Give the children their pieces of card and time to prepare their words and pictures. Encourage them to make their title

3

Building a model of a home

card first by writing the word *Homes* in large colourful letters. Then tell them to choose an interesting home to draw and label on each card, including the reverse if they have time. For example, they might choose a tent, a cave and an igloo. While the children are preparing their cards, give them, in turns, the opportunity to try out the different fastening methods. Some children might like to extend their chain with a greater selection of homes.

When the cards are complete, the children can choose different methods to attach them to each other. If appropriate, show the children how to attach a loop of wool, tape or fine string to the back of the top card using sticky tape, so that the decoration can be hung up. Alternatively, use clothes pegs as a method of attaching two materials.

Differentiation
Children:
■ decorate cards and with help find a method of attaching them to make a chain
■ decorate cards to show types of homes and demonstrate different methods of attaching them to make a chain
■ decorate cards with named drawings of homes, demonstrating a range of methods of linking them together.

Plenary
Talk about the finished decorations. Which method of joining do the children think is the most successful? Which one did they most enjoy doing? Which method would they use another time – perhaps when making a Christmas decoration?

Display
Hang all the children's decorations from a line or rail so they can be admired and discussed.

ACTIVITY 3

A HOME FOR THE HOOPALOO

DESIGN & TECHNOLOGY

Learning objective
To practise joining sheet materials and 3-D containers to make a simple model.

Resources
Disassembled boxes; card; glue; masking tape; thick string; paints and painting equipment.

Preparation
Rehearse the scenario you will relate to the children about the hoopaloo bird in the activity.

Activity
Tell the children about the hoopaloo (a fictional bird). This small brown bird about the size of a blue tit, has a white tuft of feathers on its head and lives in Australia. Explain that the hoopaloo has a problem. Because of recent bush fires, there is a shortage of the material with which the hoopaloos build their homes. People want to help the hoopaloos and are considering making temporary homes for them until things are back to normal in the bush. Ask the children if they will help by producing a home which would suit these birds. Explain that each pair of hoopaloo birds likes a home for themselves when they are ready to lay their eggs, but they also like to be close to other hoopaloos. They usually make

separate homes which are joined together. The homes hang in trees. Scientists have discovered that hoopaloos prefer the colours yellow, brown and green, which probably remind them of the sun and the plants of the bush.

Discuss how the children can make a model of a home they think the hoopaloo would choose. Have some materials to hand and encourage the children to make suggestions as to how the problem can be tackled. Perhaps boxes on top of each other would be a good idea. How will they be fastened together? How will the hoopaloos get into their homes? Where will the entrances be? How big should they be made? How should the homes be painted? What method can be used to attach them to a tree? If appropriate, sketch some of the children's best ideas so everyone understands what they are aiming for.

Ask the children to help decide what is the best order in which to do things. This could be:
1. Select materials and place them together to get an idea of what the home will be like.
2. Make the entrances for the hoopaloos either by drawing on the boxes or cutting out shapes, which could be circles or semicircles, on the same face for each box or different faces.
3. Find a way to fix the boxes together using the right amount of glue or masking tape.
4. Paint the homes in the colours which will attract the birds.
5. Attach a piece of string so that the homes can be hung in a tree.

Encourage the children to ask questions and when they are quite sure of what they are aiming for and how they will proceed they can begin to create their bird homes. Allow at least two sessions for the children to work on their models.

Differentiation
Children:
■ build a simple structure to agreed specifications, fastening boxes together with glue or masking tape
■ build a structure to specifications, cutting out entrance holes, fastening the components together and finishing appropriately
■ build a structure to specifications, adding extra detail, fixing components together, finishing and providing a method for hanging.

Plenary
Discuss the models when they are finished. Which ones do the children think suit the requirements of the hoopaloos best? Comment on the structures of the models. Are they sturdy, do they look attractive?

Display
Hang the models in a corner of the classroom accompanied by a brief outline of the story of the unfortunate hoopaloo and the specifications to which the children have worked. Perhaps some children will be prompted to make model birds to add to the display.

3

Building a model of a home

ACTIVITY 4

DESIGN & TECHNOLOGY

BUILDING FROM KITS

Learning objective
To use components from a construction kit to practise making a framework in preparation for making a model home.

Resources
A range of construction kits which use bricks, blocks, rods and straws including connectors and corner joiners; models of different houses; pictures of models and of houses being constructed; books about house building.

Preparation
Decide on the organisation of children and equipment. Working in pairs (or perhaps small groups) is probably most appropriate for this activity so that children can discuss strategies with each other as they proceed. Decide how the equipment will be shared out among the groups. You may find it useful to restrict the components of a kit allowing the children to select from a limited supply. If different kits are available, the children will produce varied examples, providing greater discussion.

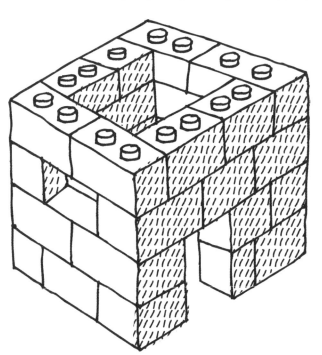

Activity
Explain to the children that people who design and build houses use models to try out their ideas because they need to know before they start on a real project how things will turn out. If they find they have made mistakes, they can easily try again. Designers probably try out lots of ideas before they are satisfied that the model shows them what they want to build. Point out that models are also a good way of showing others what a finished building will look like. Refer to previous models the children may have worked on such as the Victorian room in 'Making a model room' in section 2, and the activity 'A home for the hoopaloo', above.

Tell the children that you want them to work with a partner, or in small groups, to practise building the framework for a house using components from a construction kit. Talk about the shapes involved referring to activity 3 in section 1, if appropriate. What is the best shape for the walls? Does it matter what the shape of the base is? Encourage the children to focus on the framework of the building selecting their components from the limited supply you have provided. Do not insist on a roof at this stage and give the children the opportunity to try out their ideas without too much direction. Encourage useful collaboration between the partners, or group members, so that they respect each other's ideas and assistance.

Differentiation
Children:
■ use components from kits to make a basic framework to represent part of a house
■ use components from kits to make a framework representing a house, considering shape and proportion
■ use components from kits to create the framework of a home, adding extra parts such as interior divisions or a garage.

Plenary
Arrange the models where they can easily be seen so that the children can explain their ideas to each other. Comment on the shapes used as well as the proportions. Which models are beginning to look like a house shape? Do they all have a base? Will any have more than one storey? Which are the most stable? Will some need extra support? If there is a roof, are the walls strong enough to support it?

Display
Arrange any models and pictures of model homes together with books showing how houses are built.

ACTIVITY 5

MAKING A MODEL MORE STABLE

DESIGN & TECHNOLOGY

Learning objective
To find different ways of making the framework of a model more stable.

Resources
Construction kit components; cardboard corners; card; masking tape; scissors; photocopiable page 46; pencils and crayons.

Preparation
Select the components of the kits for each pair of children. If appropriate, prepare triangular card shapes which the children can use to make their structures more stable.

Activity
If appropriate, remind the children about their attempts at making a model framework in the 'Building from kits' activity, above. Point out that one of the most important aspects of building is to create a stable framework. Explain that a stable framework feels firm and strong and will not collapse. Refer to a climbing frame or similar structure the children are familiar with.

Examine the components belonging to different construction kits. Which parts are specially designed for making a structure more stable? How can they be used? How useful are they when building a house model? Why are they made as they are? Ask for any other good ideas for making structures stable. You could refer to ideas used in the previous activity, 'Building from kits', and consider new ways, perhaps using shapes specially made from card for corner supports. Children could try using hinges to see if that is a successful method of making their structure more stable. If appropriate, consider methods of supporting a roof. Do the walls need strengthening to prevent the framework collapsing?

Give the children the opportunity in pairs, to try out different methods of making a framework more stable. They can make a new framework each time, or try out several methods on part of a framework. Point out the importance of collaboration and encourage the children to talk to each other about their ideas as they experiment. Emphasise how useful it is to have tried out lots of different ways. When the children have had some time to work independently, bring them together to discuss their progress so far. Select some examples; encourage the children to explain and demonstrate their ideas. Why do they work so well? Could they be improved? Allow further time for investigating, if appropriate.

Recording
Provide the children with photocopiable page 46 on which they can record two successful examples. Ask them to draw the two ideas, perhaps one of their own and one of someone

3

Building a
model of a
home

else's they think is particularly good. They should write words or sentences commenting on the chosen ideas.

Differentiation

Children:
■ show a method of making a structure stable
■ collaborate to show methods of creating a stable structure, writing comments with words or simple sentences
■ collaborate to show a range of methods of making a structure stable, describing two good ideas.

Plenary

Look at examples of the children's practical and written work. Encourage them to talk about what they have learned. Why do they think their idea works so well? Could it still be improved? Praise any original ideas. Which type of construction kit makes the best components for making a framework stable? Why? Remind the children that they can use some of these ideas when making their own model.

Display

Label some examples of improving a model with comments as to how successful the children think they are. Do not always display a complete framework so as to emphasise the investigative nature of this activity and how useful it is to try out a range of ideas in preparation for making a complete model.

ACTIVITY 6

PLANNING A MODEL

DESIGN & TECHNOLOGY

Learning objective

To select materials and consider a design for a particular purpose.

Resources

A selection of disassembled boxes; different types and sizes of card; glue; masking tape; photocopiable page 47.

© 2003, Nick Dolding/alamy.com

Preparation

Collect together suitable materials the children can use for their model making. Consider the age and ability of the children and what they can achieve in the time allowed.

Activity

Explain to the children that architects are people who design buildings including houses. Before the houses can be built, the builders, as well as the people who will live in them, need to know what the house will look like. Architects and designers draw plans and make models to show people what their ideas are. They can also discover and sort out any problems which might arise when they are making the model. It would be embarrassing and expensive if there were serious problems when the real house was being built, as time and materials could be wasted.

Tell the children that they will be making a model house and first they must draw a plan of their model. They must think about the people who will live in the house, how many there are and what rooms they will need. Will the house be one storey or two? Where will the doors be? What about the windows? Will there be a garage attached? Perhaps there ought to be a garden.

Then, talk about the making of the model and what materials will be needed. Show the children a selection of boxes and different types of card. Get the children to share ideas for using the materials. *These two boxes would make the ground floor of a house. How can they be fixed together? If this card is scored and folded to make the framework of a house, how can it be made to stand upright? What would make it stable?* Suggest the children look around when at home to search out their own boxes and so on, if they need something special for their model.

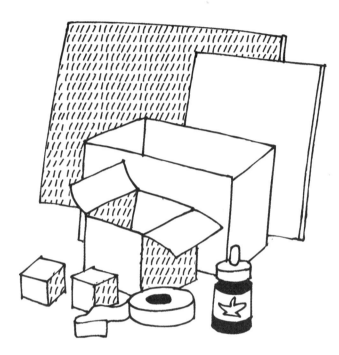

Next, discuss methods of fastening card and boxes together, referring to previous activities. Ask the children to remind each other about using materials sensibly, the right amount of glue, working efficiently and taking care with sharp tools.

If the children are to build a model with an interior, how will they let people see the details? Can a section of the model be removed, perhaps a wall or the roof? They will need to indicate this on their plan. Talk briefly about working on the details of the house. Ask for suggestions as how to represent windows, add on a chimney or aerial, whether to cover the model with paper, if it will need painting.

Before recording their plan, give the children the opportunity to look at materials and discuss ideas with a partner or adult so they are quite sure what they intend to do.

Recording
Show the children photocopiable page 47 which they can use for their recording. Some children might draw how they mean to represent the front, back and two sides of their model in the space provided; others might show only the front view.

Differentiation
Children:
■ make a picture of their proposed model indicating the materials required
■ provide a drawing and specifications for their model with details of materials required
■ provide planning details of the proposed model, including drawings of each of the four sides.

Plenary
Share some of the children's planning ideas: *Jessie's model is a bungalow. She will be able to take the roof off to show the rooms inside. Her granny and grandpa would like to live in this type of house. Sean's model is a detached house with a garden. You can peep through the windows to see the inside. He is going to fasten three boxes together for the house and use a smaller box for the garage.*

Display
Arrange models of houses made from different materials to give the children inspiration for making their own model.

3

Building a model of a home

ACTIVITY 7

DESIGN & TECHNOLOGY

MAKING A MODEL

Learning objective
To make a model for a particular purpose.

Resources
Disassembled boxes; different types of card and paper; collage materials; masking tape; glue; paints and painting equipment.

Preparation
Decide on the organisation of the sessions for the model making; provide each child with a storage area for their work, which could be a large box or tray in which the plan and materials being used are stored.

Activity
Tell the children that they are going to make the model they designed in the previous activity. Take them through the stages of making their model:

1. Encourage the children to consult their plan, collect the materials they need and begin to assemble the framework. Point out that it is a good idea to put the parts together in a temporary way at first so that it will be easier to work on any details. Perhaps at this stage they need to cut out doors and windows if that is their plan or work on the interior. There might be some painting at this stage.

2. Children might need a further session to work on the details of their model; some parts might be ready for attaching.

3. By now all the parts should be joined and fixed to the base. The children should consider if the model needs more stability. Then the finishing process can begin. If the outside is painted it will need drying time.

4. Allow the children a final session to improve their models, adding further details and finishing touches. Encourage each child to make a label for their model, which can be a simple title or short explanation.

Differentiation
Children:
■ make a simple model of a home for a particular purpose to their own specifications
■ make a model of a home, following a plan and using previously learned techniques
■ make a detailed model of a home, following a plan, with the emphasis on making the structure stable and finishing carefully.

Plenary
Admire the models. Select some children to talk about their own model and whether they are satisfied with the outcome. Is the model stable? Which part are they most pleased with? Which parts could have been better? Does it look attractive? Is it carefully finished off? Does the model meet the specifications? Would the person it was intended for be pleased with it and want the real home to be built?

Display
Arrange all the models where they can easily be seen by the children and any visitors. Display the planning sheets from the previous activity near by.

CURRICULUM LINKS ages 5–7: Houses and homes

Everyone needs a home

Somewhere to sleep safely	A place to shelter from the weather
Somewhere to keep belongings	A place to be with the family

Why I need a home

_____

_____

_____

DESIGN & TECHNOLOGY

Making a model more stable

Good idea 1

Good idea 2

Planning a model

Who will live in the house?

What do they need?

What materials and tools will I use for my model?

How will I join the materials?

This is what my model will look like.

Section 4

An island home

FOCUS

GEOGRAPHY

GEOGRAPHY
- recognising islands on a map
- features of islands
- living on an island
- travelling to and around an island
- comparing island life with life on the mainland
- how island life is changing
- asking questions and expressing opinions
- geographical vocabulary
- mapwork

HISTORY

HISTORY
- identifying different features of houses

Preparation for section 4

For most children at this stage, especially those living away from the coast, their experience of islands will be limited. With the help of the activities in this section, aim to give the children something of an island experience. Collect maps, pictures, travel brochures, video film and stories with an island theme.

Creating an island

Create an 'island' which the children can use for role-play, and devise situations based on the activities in this section to help increase their awareness of life on an island. If possible, create this island outside, either on the school field or playground. Use skipping rope or washing line to mark out the coastline and a section of mainland. On a hard surface, a more permanent outline can be made using chalk or playground paint.

If outdoor activity is not possible, use a large indoor floor space such as the hall.

Map 1. First sketch out the island to fit on a sheet of A4 paper. The shape of the island should be simple so that it can be easily marked out or assembled and reassembled several times with the help of the children. However, include some interesting coastline characteristics which will help the children remember the shape. Think of a name for the island which will appeal to the children; it could reflect the island's shape or have some relevance to the children themselves. Include a section of mainland, (along one side of the page) so the children can relate the position of the island to the mainland.

Map 2. On a copy of Map 1 mark as symbols the physical features the island will have, such as:
- coastline – cliffs and beaches
- interior – one or more hills
- a stream coming from one of the hills
- groups of trees
- rocks
- cave
- grassy slopes
- boggy places.

Also, mark these symbols on labels made from fairly large pieces of card (approximately A3 size). Use one colour to symbolise that they are physical features. The labels can be simple, large, folded pieces of card or could be fastened to canes which can be pushed into the ground or made to stand freely using a base of Plasticine or similar material.

Map 3. Decide where some human aspects of the island will be found and add these to a copy of Map 2 to make Map 3. Include a jetty and buildings such as several houses, a farmhouse, barn, boathouse, shop, school, fish store, and so on. Link the buildings with tracks or roads. As above, make large labels to represent the larger buildings. Use card of a different colour to contrast with the physical features.

Map 4. Make a large basic map of the island to display in the classroom and refer to as the activities get under way. Physical and human features can be added as appropriate.

ACTIVITY 1

GEOGRAPHY

LOOKING FOR ISLANDS

Learning objective
To identify islands on a map and globe.

Resources
A suitable rock to make a small island; a container of water; a globe; a large map of the British Isles which is suitable for children to use to identify small and larger islands; video film or photograph showing an aerial view of a small island; enlarged photocopiable page 59.

Preparation
Arrange the rock in the container of water to make a simple island. Before enlarging photocopiable page 59 for the children, mark the location of the school/home area on the simplified map of the British Isles. If appropriate, also label a limited number of larger islands, especially those which are relevant to the children's experience, such as Ireland, the Isle of Man, the Isle of Wight, Anglesey, Scottish islands and so on.

Activity
Establish that an island is a piece of land with water all around it. Show the children the island you have made using a rock and a container of water to reinforce this. Explain that islands can be all shapes and sizes. Some are almost round; others are shaped a bit like a triangle or an animal's face. Sometimes the names of islands give an idea of what shape they are, for example Long Island. Other names of islands tell you what creatures live there, for example Pigeon Island and Bear Island.

   Now, show the children a globe and explain that this represents planet Earth which we live on. The blue areas represent oceans of the world and the other coloured areas the land. As you slowly spin the globe, ask the children to decide if they can see more land or more water. Point out that there is a larger area of water covering the Earth than there is land, so there are bound to be many pieces of land we can call islands, some which seem quite large and others which are just represented by dots. Ask some children to point out islands on the globe, not necessarily naming them unless children know of friends and relations living on distant islands. If appropriate, make the comment that planet Earth would be more suitably named planet Ocean. Show the children a video film or aerial photograph of an island.

Next, show the children a large map of the British Isles. Explain that this map represents the part of the world where we live and that *isle* is another name for island. Indicate the location of the school by a small sticker. Establish which parts of the map are the areas of sea and then ask the children to begin to look for islands. Where can the children see any big islands? Where are most of the small islands? Have any of the children visited one of the islands? Is there an island near to where the children live?

Point out that Britain is an island itself in relation to mainland Europe, but is called the mainland in relation to the smaller isles around it.

Recording
Give the children photocopiable page 59, on which they can identify some of the islands and perhaps highlight and name any which have a special meaning for them. Ask the children to write a relevant sentence to accompany the map, referring to any island they know of or have perhaps visited. For example, *My auntie has been to the Isle of Wight for her holidays; Scotland has a lot of islands.*

Differentiation
Children:
■ identify islands on a globe and map
■ identify islands on a globe and recognise the mainland and some islands on a map of the British Isles, adding relevant words or sentences
■ identify islands on a globe, and the mainland and significant islands on a map of the British Isles, adding sentences relating to islands they know.

Display
Display the large map of the British Isles with some of the islands named and highlighted, such as the ones children might have visited, any near to the school's location or which have taken the children's attention.

Plenary
Ask the children to remind each other how they would recognise an island on a map. Can they remember the location and names of any of the islands they have talked about in this activity?

ACTIVITY 2

PHYSICAL FEATURES OF AN ISLAND

GEOGRAPHY

Learning objectives
To be aware of physical features an island might have and how to record these on a map; to understand how an island differs from the mainland.

Resources
Maps 1 and 2 (see Preparation for section 4, page 48); rope or chalk to make the outline of island; labels and/or markers with symbols of the physical features listed for Map 2; photocopiable page 60.

Preparation
Mark out the plan of the island on Map 1 on the field/playground/hall beforehand, if possible.

Include part of the mainland. Use points of reference so that the children can help recreate the plan for other activities.

Activity

Show the children the island you have drawn (Map 1). Explain that this map shows an island which you have set out on the school field/playground/hall floor and will be using to help them understand what islands are like. The outline of the island will be like a map and together you will try to show the special features of the island. No one lives there so everything on the island is natural; nothing is made by people.

Take the children outside/to the hall to see the island. Ask them to sit on the mainland. Make sure all the children understand that what they can see is a larger version of the island you showed them on Map 1, with the rope or chalk representing the coastline. Establish which parts are land and which is the sea. Point out that the mainland stretches much further away behind where they are sitting. Make a special announcement to give the island its name, perhaps using ceremonial terms and ringing a bell. Encourage them to use this name when talking about the island.

Show the children the labels which represent the physical features and together decide where these features could be on the island. First, give a child a marker representing a beach and direct them to where you have decided the best access to the island will be. Other children can position markers along the coastline to represent cliffs. Next, put in the stream and then discuss the island's other interior features by finding the positions of hills, groups of trees, rocks, grassy and boggy places. Each time direct a child to the pre-planned position of each feature, using Map 2 as a guide. Point out to the children that they have made a plan of the island, as it would appear on a map. Before returning to the classroom, tell the children that you will be visiting the island again and need to remember its shape and position so that the plan can be recreated quickly. Briefly establish the extent of the plan and its position in relation to surrounding features, such as the edge of the playground, part of a building or a nearby tree.

Recording

Depending on the ability of the children and the time available, give them copies of the island map (Map 1) and ask them to draw in the features as symbols, using this basic outline. Otherwise provide them with copies of Map 2 with the symbol features already in place. Point out that the symbols represent the features they used earlier and a key is required to explain what the symbols represent. Give the children photocopiable page 60 for them to complete the key. Explain that the key symbols they draw must be the same as those used on the map.

Differentiation

Children:
- recognise some physical features of an island and relate symbols on a map to a key
- recognise physical features of an island, drawing symbols on a map and completing a key
- recognise physical features of an island, complete a map and provide a key.

Plenary

Look at the finished maps and emphasise that the features included are all physical, that is, natural. Ask questions which require the children to use the key when providing their answers: *Where on this plan can we find rocks? What is the symbol for a boggy place? We need to know so we can avoid that part of the island.*

© NASA/Getty Images

Display

Display the children's work and perhaps a large version of Map 2 displayed horizontally on a table.

GEOGRAPHY

HISTORY

ACTIVITY 3

HUMAN FEATURES OF AN ISLAND

Learning objectives
To identify human features of an island; to recap on features of homes.

Resources
The plan of the island and mainland from Map 2; markers to represent the physical features as used in the previous activity; copies of Map 2; pencils and crayons.

Preparation
Make new markers to represent the human features of the island – two or three houses, jetty, shop, fish store, boathouse, community building, school. These markers should be of a different shape or colour to distinguish them from the physical features markers. Recreate the outdoor/large island from activity 2, with the markers representing the physical features in place.

Activity
Take the children to the site of the recreated island. Refer to the labels identifying the physical features from the previous activity. What do the children think they would need if they were going to live on the island? Talk about a shelter. Perhaps the children think a tent would be a good idea. Other children may want to build a house. Remind the children about tides, inaccessible places which might be steep or boggy, all of which will need to be avoided. Ask some children to consider a good place for a home. Do the others agree? Is the spot far enough away from the sea? Is it too near a boggy or steep part of the island? Will there be a good view towards the mainland or out to sea? Ask the children to add markers where they have agreed would be good places to build homes on the island.

If appropriate, remind them of earlier activities on different types of homes. What sort of features do they think houses built on this island might have? Perhaps a chimney, as they may have to burn coal or wood fires (point out that there would be no electricity on the island). Ask the children to consider what materials the houses might be built from, reminding them that they may have to use materials on the island itself, so perhaps local stone may be appropriate.

Talk about essential items they will need to take with them to live on the island, such as food and water or means of getting them, means of cooking, suitable clothing and bedding, medicines and first aid kit. Then think about other items which they would like to take, such as books, games and so on. Remind the children that there is no electricity on this small island.

Next, consider changes which might take place if more people decided to live on the island. As well as needing more homes, what else might be required? Suggest a jetty which enables the ferry to land goods and people more easily, a shop, fish store and boathouse. Point out that eventually the islanders would want a school and a community building where they can get together for various events. Use the new markers to indicate where the buildings might be. Point out that to get from the jetty to people's homes and from their homes to other buildings tracks will be made which will become small roads.

Recording
Back in the classroom, ask the children to describe buildings other than homes which they think will be needed on an island. On a copy of Map 2 they can show where they think these extra buildings might be and link them with tracks or roads.

Differentiation
Children:
■ are aware of some of the features which develop on an island when people live there

- describe the buildings and other features which develop on an island when people live there
- describe the human features which develop on an island and add these to a map.

Plenary
Distinguish between the island's natural (physical) features and the features which arise from people living there. Ask the children to recall the human influences on the island.

Display
Add symbols to Map 4 to show where the homes and other buildings are located.

ACTIVITY 4

GEOGRAPHY

ISLANDERS TRAVELLING

Learning objective
To identify suitable means of transport when living on a small island.

Resources
Pictures and video film showing ferries and other boats taking people and cargo to an island and tractors as well as lorries and bicycles to show ways of travelling around the island; the plan of the island from activities 2 and 3 (optional); paper; pencils and crayons.

Preparation
Rehearse some scenarios which require people to travel to and from an island or around an island.

© 2003, Sindre Ellingsen/alamy.com

Activity
Refer to the island in activities 2 and 3, if appropriate, and talk about reaching the island from the mainland. Explain that a ferry is a boat which takes people and goods across a short stretch of water and is very important to islanders. Show pictures of ferries from holiday brochures or a video film, if available. Tell the children that a small ferry would be most suitable to link a small island with the mainland. Ask the children what they think would need to be delivered regularly to an island. Discuss food supplies, post and other goods. Point out that not everything is useful or suitable to have on an island, for instance a sports car would not be a good idea on a small island.

Move on to talk about how the people get around their island. As distances are small, walking is the obvious choice. The children will suggest that a bicycle might be useful where the land is fairly flat. How will large items be moved? Discuss the lack of roads and that paths and tracks are the only routes. What vehicles do the children suggest? A vehicle which can survive rough conditions and is good for carrying things would be useful, however.

Present the children with some scenarios and ask them to suggest the most suitable transport methods for each case. If appropriate, take the children to the recreated island from activities 2 and 3 and enact some of the situations. For example:
- Lucy's friend wants to visit her on the island. How will she get there?
- A family decide they will do some farming on the island and need a tractor. How will a tractor be delivered to the island?

■ Sandeep breaks his leg while playing on the rocks. What will happen next?
■ A boat brings supplies to the island. How do the islanders get the goods to their homes?
■ Molly is going fishing from a beach on the other side of the island, how will she get there?

Recording
The children can write words or sentences about, and draw, methods of travelling to and from the island as well as ways of travelling around the island itself, perhaps linking their work to the scenario examples.

Differentiation
Children:
■ describe, using pictures and words, travelling to, from and around a small island
■ describe, using drawings and sentences, how people travel to, from and around a small island
■ write an account of the travelling methods used by islanders and visitors getting to and from and around a small island.

Plenary
Ask the children why people do not usually have cars on a small island. What are the best ways of getting around for people and for heavy goods? Emphasise that a ferry is very important to island people as it brings vital supplies as well as visitors.

Display
Arrange the pictures showing transport methods along with the children's recording.

ACTIVITY 5

WORKING ON AN ISLAND

GEOGRAPHY

Learning objective
To be aware that living on a small island determines the work people do.

© 2003, Bernd Mellmann/alamy.com

Resources
Pictures showing the types of work done on a small island, especially fishing, farming and ferry operating; paper; pencils and crayons.

Preparation
On cards, write the types of jobs people have, both islanders and people on the mainland, including fisherman, farmer, ferryman, shopkeeper, teacher, doctor, dentist, mechanic, car park attendant, crossing warden, baker. Prepare the island again, positioning the markers from Map 3 on it.

Activity
Ask the children what work they think people on a small island might be able or need to do. First they might think of the more obvious jobs like fishing and farming.

Talk about how these activities can help the people who do them as well as other people on the island and the mainland.

Then give examples of work done in the children's own neighbourhood and ask if this job could be done on a small island. *Sasha's mum is a traffic warden. Would there be any work for her to do on a small island? Tim's dad is a train driver. Would he find work there?* Refer to places in the children's local area where people work, such as shopping centres, factories, restaurants. Remind the children that these are not found on a small island, because there

would not be enough people to work in them or need them. Because there are not many people living on the island there may not be enough work for a doctor or a dentist. Then talk about the services the island people would require regularly. Someone would need to operate a ferry, run a small shop, deliver letters, teach the children. Point out that on an island one person often does several jobs. The post person might also be a shopkeeper and the ferry operator could also be a fisherman.

After the discussion, take the children out to the recreated island and ask them to sit on the mainland. Draw attention to the markers which show the positions of the buildings. Point out that some of the jobs people do will be connected with these buildings. In turn, ask some children to select one of the cards which indicate a type of work. The children then decide whether this job can be done on the island. If they think a teacher is needed for

2003, Ken Gillham/alamy.com

the school, the child with the card can make the journey to the island. Children with cards of jobs which are not possible on the island stay on the mainland. Some jobs will require the children to discuss and make decisions. For example, will there be enough work for a mechanic on the island? Perhaps islanders will have to catch the ferry when they need to see a doctor or nurse.

Recording

Back in the classroom, ask the children to write about or draw the job or jobs they would do if they were living on the island. They could perhaps comment on work they would like to do but is not possible on the island.

Differentiation

Children:
- describe island jobs using drawings and words
- describe island jobs using drawings and providing comments in sentences
- explain why certain jobs are suitable for islanders while others are only possible on the mainland.

Plenary

Remind the children that there are only certain types of work which can be done on an island. Ask for some examples of jobs which are impossible to do there. Why do the children think that some people have to do several part-time jobs?

Display

Display the children's accounts together with pictures of people doing a variety of jobs.

4

An island
home

GEOGRAPHY

COMPARING COMMUNITIES

Learning objective
To recognise differences and similarities between island life and that of the children's local community.

Resources
Board or flip chart; pencils and crayons; paper.

Preparation
Depending on the locality, decide on the aspects upon which to focus. Look for obvious contrasts or similarities between rural/urban/seaside communities; quiet, peaceful places or busy, noisy places. Draw two large oval shapes on the board with a title 'How living on a small island is different from living in Xxx.'

Activity
Begin by asking the children for some differences they have noticed between island life and that of their own community. Discuss their general ideas first. Then begin to group the differences. Show the children the two shapes you have prepared. Into the first, collect their ideas relating to people, such as more people in their community, more buildings, more traffic. In the second shape, include differences to do with the landscape and surroundings.
  Then discuss what is similar in each community and make a special list. Perhaps both communities are by the sea; both are small; certain jobs are possible in both neighbourhoods; people in each community have places where they can meet and make friends.

Recording
Ask the children to describe the differences between their community and that on a small island. They could write an account, make lists or present their ideas using drawings.

Differentiation
Children:
■ indicate using drawings and words some differences and similarities between their own community and that on a small island
■ describe by drawing and writing sentences the differences and similarities between their own community and that on a small island
■ write an account describing differences and similarities between their own community and that on a small island.

Plenary
Emphasise that although the children might have discovered lots of differences between their community and one on a small island, there are similarities in that people need to live together in a friendly way, meeting, helping each other and making friends. Do the children think there are more differences than similarities or vice versa?

Display
Display the children's work with pictures and photographs of the differences between their community and island life.

ACTIVITY 7

GEOGRAPHY

WOULD YOU LIKE TO LIVE ON A SMALL ISLAND?

An island
home

Learning objective
To express views and give opinions on the
likes and dislikes of a place.

Resources
Board or flip chart; paper; pencils and
crayons.

Activity
Ask the children to tell you, now they know
quite a lot about life on a small island, what
they would like most about living on one.
Perhaps they will talk about living by the sea
and playing on the beach. Perhaps they will
enjoy the peaceful atmosphere and the lovely
scenery, not having to worry about traffic
and crossing busy roads. They might like the
idea of belonging to a small community and
getting to know everybody.

Then ask the children what they would miss
most and what things would be difficult to do if they lived on a small island. Do they agree
on the things they feel they could not do without? On the board, make a list of ten things the
class would miss the most. Talk about having to travel to the mainland to go to the cinema
and hospital and to visit friends and relatives. This might take a long time so perhaps would
not happen often. Discuss the type and size of school the children would go to on a small
island. Would they mind not having so many other children to talk to and play with, make up
a football team and so on? Briefly mention wintertime and the storms and wind people on
the island might experience.

Recording
Ask the children to write a personal account describing what they would like about island life
and what they would miss the most. Ask them to decide where they would like to live – on
the island or in their own community.

Differentiation
Children:
■ express their own views in words and pictures about life on an island
■ express their own views, writing sentences to describe their opinions of island life
■ present a reasoned argument indicating their ideas about where they would like to live.

Plenary
Tell the class what the majority have decided; whether there are many who would like to go
and live on an island, whether most would prefer to stay in a familiar place. Perhaps some
children would like to live for a time on an island but return after a while. Point out that
everyone's views should be respected, that not everyone has the same feelings and ideas.

Display
Make two display areas presenting the ideas of those children who would like to live on an
island and those who prefer the place where they live at present.

4

An island home

GEOGRAPHY

ACTIVITY 8

A CHANGING ENVIRONMENT

Learning objective
To recognise that changes occur in an environment.

Resources
Pictures showing changes to island life, such as the building of houses and roads, vehicles; the island recreated in previous activities (optional).

Activity
Tell the children that changes are always taking place in any environment. Briefly refer to changes which the children can see are happening near by, perhaps new houses or a road being built, recently planted trees, a building being demolished. Ask the children what changes will take place on an island and use pictures to help them identify changes. Remind them of the island you created outside/in the hall and ask what changes occurred when people went to live there. They should mention building houses, making paths and tracks, using the land for farming and other activities which provide work. Talk about the rubbish created by people living on the island and the problems this creates. What will people on islands do with anything they no longer need? Do the children consider the changes are good or bad? They are good for the people who need homes and work but perhaps not so good for the island itself and the wild creatures who already live there.

Discuss why only a few people can live on a small island. What would happen if it became crowded? Would there be space to build enough houses? Would there be sufficient supplies to go around? Would everyone have a job? It would not be quiet and peaceful any longer.

Explain that often people decide to move to the mainland where they can find work and have access to things people on the mainland take for granted. Imagine everyone leaving the island the children have come to know through the previous activities. If appropriate, take the children to the recreated island one last time. With a group of children, enact the settlers leaving and returning to the mainland. Talk about the changes which they have made while living on the island. What will be left behind? The houses and any other buildings will be still there, the pathways and tracks will remain. Will there be unwanted belongings? Will the island be the special place it was before anyone arrived?

Differentiation
Children:
■ are aware of some of the human influences on an environment

■ discuss how people make environmental changes within a community
■ recognise changes people make within communities and discuss the benefits and problems they cause.

Plenary
Emphasise that changes are always taking place, especially where there are people living. Point out that every community sees changes, the one the children are a part of as much as that on a small island. Discuss how unwanted changes, such as disturbing native animals might be avoided.

GEOGRAPHY

Photocopiable

Looking for islands

Find the islands. Can you name any?

_____

_____

_____

■SCHOLASTIC

GEOGRAPHY

Physical features of an island

Complete the key.

beach	hills	boggy places
cliffs	rocks	grassy slopes
cave	trees	stream

Display

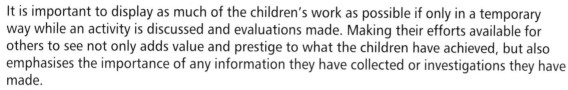

It is important to display as much of the children's work as possible if only in a temporary way while an activity is discussed and evaluations made. Making their efforts available for others to see not only adds value and prestige to what the children have achieved, but also emphasises the importance of any information they have collected or investigations they have made.

If children know that their work will be valued and available for others to see, they will take more care over presentation. At this stage of their development, the habit of always producing their best efforts can be encouraged.

Individual presentation

Collect each child's individual work – drawings, completed worksheets, written pieces and so on – and present them in a folder or as a booklet which they can personalise and show to each other and their parents. If necessary, any pieces of work needed for a classroom display can be photocopied.

Provide photocopies of pictures, such as a typical Victorian home or an aerial photograph of an island, which the children can add to their work to give the folders or booklets an extra dimension.

Classroom display

Begin to build up a display as soon as the work on *Houses and homes* begins. The displays will evolve over the weeks as the work progresses.

It can be useful to display each child's work relating to any specific activity, in a temporary way, perhaps with Blu-Tack, so that discussion and evaluation can take place and the work can be admired.

Where appropriate, photocopy and enlarge examples of individuals' work to use with a display.

If space is limited in the classroom, extend the display into the corridor or school hall.

Frequently refer to the displays as the topic progresses, using them for reference and information.

The activities in *Houses and homes* lend themselves to four separate but linked areas of display: Homes: now and then; Inside homes: now and then; Building a model of a home; and An island home. The theme of each can be emphasised by a certain colour scheme, appropriate lettering or particular arrangement of material.

Suggestions for display for each section
Homes: now and then

■ Begin by building up a display of pictures and photographs of different types of homes and including the list of homes to which the children will add examples. Make labels or captions to describe the homes.

■ Extend the display to show features of homes, referring to the mathematical shapes the children have discovered, and old and new homes. Include the photo-montage of different doors/windows/chimneys (see page 7 of Getting started).

Inside homes: now and then

■ Use pictures, photographs, books and so on to show the interior of homes about a hundred years ago.

Identify different rooms and highlight the children's comments to add to the display.
■ Arrange any artefacts relating to home activities of Victorian/Edwardian times with captions or short explanations about how they were used. Use pictures of large items such as furniture and kitchen equipment.
■ If appropriate, prepare a corner of the classroom to represent a Victorian/Edwardian room where the children can handle artefacts and involve themselves in role-play.
■ Display the model rooms the children have made, so that they can be easily seen and discussed.

Building a model of a home
■ Hang the chains depicting homes from a rail or line. These could be displayed with the work and information on different homes from section 1.
■ The homes the children have created for the hoopaloos can be suspended around the classroom with an accompanying explanation.

■ If space allows, organise a section of the classroom as a workshop to accommodate a range of construction kits which the children can use when trying out their ideas for making stable structures. Have an area near by where successful examples can be displayed with short descriptions.
■ When the model homes are completed, considerable space in the classroom will be required to display them all. Try to display the planning sheets alongside each model. It is important to try to find space for everyone's designs and models.

An island home
■ Display a map of the British Isles with some of the islands highlighted.
■ Arrange pictures of islands and island life to accompany the activities in this section. Include travelling and working activities. Make available books of stories with an island theme.
■ Display the large map of the island you create in section 4 (Map 4; see page 49).
■ Arrange the children's maps, their opinions of island life and the comparisons they make with their own homes and communities.

Assessment

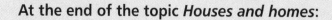

At the end of the topic *Houses and homes*:

HISTORY
■ Can the children identify different types of homes in their locality?
■ Can they recognise the differences between new and older houses?
■ Can they make relevant observations relating to the features of homes?
■ Are they aware of some differences between their own home life and that of a hundred years ago?
■ Do they understand how household items affect the way we live?
■ Can they communicate through speaking, drawing and writing what they have learned about houses and homes?

DESIGN AND TECHNOLOGY
■ Are they aware that everyone needs a home?
■ Can the children recognise and name basic mathematical shapes in the context of houses and homes?
■ Can they use skills and techniques they have learned to join 2-D and 3-D materials together to make models?
■ Can they use their own experiences of houses and homes when developing their ideas?
■ Can they evaluate their models, making relevant comments?

GEOGRAPHY
■ Can the children identify islands on a map?
■ Do they understand that the features of a place can be represented as symbols on a map or plan?
■ Do they recognise some of the advantages and disadvantages of living on a small island?
■ Can they make relevant comments and give their opinions on an island home?
■ Have they increased their geographical vocabulary?

Drawing the topic to a close

Look back with the children at what has been achieved throughout the work on *Houses and homes*. Point out how much they have learned, all the information they have gathered, the enjoyment they have had. Remind them of the observations they have made, the models they have constructed and the island activities they have been involved in. Ask the children to tell you which part of the topic they have enjoyed the most and which piece(s) of work they are most proud of.

Arrange a simple but special event as a finale. This could be a picture quiz which the children help to organise themselves. Show pictures and ask the children questions relating to *Houses and homes*: *Is this a new house or an older one? What is this household item used for? What job is this person doing on the island?* Some children might like to devise their own questions for the rest of the class.

Re-enact a five-minute scene relating to one aspect of the topic, such as a Victorian household activity or a scenario typical of island life. The performance could be presented to the rest of the school during assembly time or for parents when they come to view the displays of the children's work.